The Corning Collection

Quick Recipes for Simply Delicious Meals

Volume 2
Featuring Pyrex® Bakeware

Step by Step Books, Inc.
NEW YORK • TORONTO

Preface

Cooking is many things, but most of all it should be fun. From a one-course salad to a many course feast, the job of the chef is to bring out and enhance the flavors, the aromas, and the colors of each ingredient alone, and each dish as it combines these ingredients into something more. A gourmet meal doesn't have to mean a complex meal. Rather it can be a very simple meal that tastes great and looks beautifully. Gourmet simply means bringing out the best of each dish

There arc three keys to successful cooking. First, plan your overall meal from start to finish. Think how each course goes together, and how much time each will need to bc completed. Don't take on more than you have time to complete. Second, read each recipe fully. You don't want to get halfway through a recipe and find out that you are unable to complete it. Third, organize your ingredients before you begin. Be sure you have each one at hand, in the proper quantity and prepared as noted in each recipe.

One final key to good cooking: Be sure to buy the freshest ingredients possible. Make sure that the colors of your ingredients are intense and deep; that they are the proper texture; and that they have not been sitting in the stores too long, The fresher the ingredients, the better your meal will be.

So start cooking! You'll find these tempting, easy-to-create recipes perfect for the beginning or more advanced cook And remember: Have Fun!

Table of Contents

iv. Getting Started
Planning Ahead

I. Appetizers
Crudites	6
Ginger-Lime Vinaigrette with Crudities	7
Curry Dip for Crudities	8
Herbed Olives	8

II. Salads, Soups, & Stews
Winter Holiday Salad	9
Minted Cucumber	10
Spinach and Marinated Mushroom Salad	11
Fruited Chicken Salad	12
Hearty Mediterranean Soup	14
Potato-Plus Soup	15

III. Poultry
Japanese Chicken, Carrots, and Parsnips	16
Roasted Turkey	18
Wild Rice Stuffing a L'Orange	20
Fresh Cranberry-Orange Relish	21
Curried Chicken-Broccoli Casserole	22

IV. Fish
Hot Snapper Veracruz	23
Fillet of Sole with Tomatoes and Parsley	24
Halibut with Confetti Sauce	25
Creamy Non-Dairy Pimento Sauce	25

V. Meat
Grilled Lamb Kebabs	27
Roast Leg of Spring Lamb	28
Baja Tacos	29
Peppers and Steak	30

VI. Vegetables
Broccoli, Carrot and Spanish Timbales	33
Corn Pudding	34
New Cottage Potatoes	35
Steamed Zucchini and Tomatoes	35
Baked Tomato Provencale	36
Winter Vegetable Potpourri	38
Red Onion Preserves	40

VII. Beans/Rice/Pasta/Grains
Fruitta Di Mare Pasta	42
Presto Pizza	44
Angel Hair Pasta and Artichokes	46
Red Pepper Sauce	48
Pumpkin Bread	50
Italian Bread with Olive Oil and Herbs	51
Banana Fig Bread	52

VIII. Desserts
Chocolate Angel Food Cake	54
Raspberry Sauce	55
Chocolate Torte	56
Iced Winter Fruit	58
Poached Pears	60
Ginger Cookies	61
Royal Meringues	62
Rhubarb Crisp	64

Plan Ahead

Cooking a simple meal or a gourmet feast can be easy and fun for the chef—with just a little advance planning. The keys to success are organization and preparation.

First and foremost, plan your meal—the number of courses, types of food, and recipes. In choosing the menu, keep in mind your cooking skills and the time required to prepare the ingredients and cook.

To expand your cooking repertoire, try out new recipes and techniques on family and very close friends first rather than on guests. That alone will eliminate a lot of stress and anxiety. When entertaining, cook and serve dishes that you already know how to make.

Getting Started

You've shopped, the ingredients are on hand, and you're ready to begin. Here are two absolute rules to follow before you start cooking that will make your time in the kitchen more fun and rewarding:

1. Always read the recipe through.
2. Assemble all the ingredients, cleaned, prepared, and measured.

Here's a tip to help avoid mistakes and omissions: For each recipe, clean, prepare, and measure the ingredients and place them on a tray. In the case of ingredients that must be kept refrigerated, write the name of each ingredient on a separate card and put the cards on the tray. This may seem simplistic, but try it—you won't leave anything out Also, keep in mind that, to save time, many items can be cleaned, prepared, and measured while other ingredients are cooking.

I. APPETIZERS

CRUDITES

Crudités, raw or blanched vegetables or fruits, are universally popular—and healthy, too! But don't feel constrained. Why not try some of the following with your favorite dips and sauces?

> Apple slices
> Beet slices
> Daikon radish slices
> Jicama slices
> Pear slices
>
> Red cabbage, crisp slices
> Tiny new potatoes, steamed and sliced
> Snow peas, blanched
> Sugar snap peas, blanched

Ginger-Lime Vinaigrette with Crudités

Use as a dip for asparagus, green beans, broccoli, carrots, cauliflower, daikon, snow peas, or zucchini. Serve as a dressing for artichokes.

INGREDIENTS:
- ¼ cup grated fresh ginger
- 4 scallions, white and tender greens, minced
- ½ cup fresh lime juice
- ¼ cup light sesame oil
- ¼ cup soy sauce
- ¾ cup vegetable oil
- Toasted sesame seeds (optional)

EQUIPMENT:
- Small (1-quart) mixing bowl

Combine all ingredients except sesame seeds in bowl and whisk together. Refrigerate overnight. Add toasted sesame seeds just before serving or serve separately in a saucer in which the moistened vegetables can be dipped. *Yield: about 2 cups.*

Curry Dip for Crudités

Less fat and tastier than a mayonnaise-based dip, serve it with crudités, cold artichoke, or asparagus.

INGREDIENTS:
8 ounces farmer's cheese
¼ cup nonfat buttermilk
1 tablespoon fresh lemon juice
1 small onion, minced
1 garlic clove, minced
1 tablespoon curry powder
1 teaspoon chili powder

EQUIPMENT:
Food processor or blender

Process the farmer's cheese, buttermilk, and lemon juice in food processor or blender until smooth. Add remaining ingredients and process until well blended. Chill overnight to blend flavors. *Yield about 1 cup.*

TIP: To smooth the curry-powder flavor, mix it with lemon juice in a glass cup and microwave on MEDIUM power for 30 seconds. Let cool before adding to processor.

Herbed Olives

INGREDIENTS:
½ cup olive oil
1 tablespoon red-wine vinegar
1 tablespoon chopped garlic
1 tablespoon chopped fresh rosemary leaves or
1½ teaspoons dried rosemary
Freshly ground black pepper to taste
2 pounds large Greek olives, black and green

TIP: Olives will keep refrigerated for several weeks.

Combine first five ingredients in bowl, mix well, add olives, and toss until well coated. Cover and marinate for at least 24 hours, stirring occasionally. Serve at room temperature. *Yield: about 6 cups.*

II. Salads, Soups & Stews

Winter Holiday Salad

Adding the dressing ahead of time lets the watercress wilt slightly and blends flavors nicely. It's a perfect make-ahead dish for the holiday chef who wants to spend more time with family and guests.

Toss all salad ingredients together in salad bowl. Whisk together oil and vinegar; add salt and pepper to taste; pour dressing over salad and refrigerate at least 1 hour before serving. *Serves 8.*

INGREDIENTS:
2 small heads red cabbage, cored and coarsely chopped
4 bunches watercress, coarsely chopped
2 heads Belgian endive, base trimmed and coarsely chopped
12 scallions, white and tender greens, chopped
2 red or Granny Smith apples, unpeeled, cored, and sliced
8 ounces Stilton cheese, crumbled

DRESSING:
1 cup walnut oil
1/3 cup red-wine, raspberry, or cider vinegar
Salt and freshly ground black pepper to taste

EQUIPMENT:
Salad bowl
Small bowl or 2-cup measuring cup

Minted Cucumber

This delightful accompaniment to beef dishes is also terrific with spicy foods.

INGREDIENTS:
1 tablespoon sugar
1 cup warm water
1 cup white-wine vinegar
Salt and freshly ground white pepper to taste
1 long seedless cucumber, peeled and sliced very thin
½ cup chopped mint leaves

EQUIPMENT:
Bowl or refrigerator storage container

In bowl, dissolve sugar in warm water; add water and vinegar. Whisk and add mint and cucumbers. Cover and refrigerate at least 3 hours, but not more than 6. Drain cucumbers before serving. *Serves 6.*

Spinach and Marinated Mushroom Salad

The marinated mushrooms are healthier than the traditional bacon and hard-cooked eggs usually served in spinach salads.

INGREDIENTS:
1 cup water
1 pound small fresh mushrooms, trimmed and halved
3 large garlic cloves, mashed
1 bay leaf
½ teaspoon dried thyme
½ teaspoon dried, crushed rosemary
¼ teaspoon dried marjoram
Salt and freshly ground black pepper to taste
Juice of ½ lemon
½ cup olive oil
¾ cup wine vinegar
2 pounds spinach

EQUIPMENT:
Small bowl or 2-cup measuring cup
Salad bowl

Bring 1 cup water to a boil; add mushrooms, cover, and boil 2 minutes. Drain and place in glass bowl. Whisk together remaining ingredients except spinach in small bowl and blend well. Pour over hot mushrooms and chill at least 1 hour. Tear spinach into bite-sized pieces and place in salad bowl. Add mushrooms and enough marinade to dress, but not drown, greens. Toss lightly and serve. *Serves 8.*

Fruited Chicken Salad with Raspberry Vinaigrette

To make vinaigrette, whisk together olive oil, vinegar, salt, and pepper and blend well. Cut *cooked* chicken into bite-sized or larger pieces. Toss chicken, apple slices, grapes, and walnuts with vinaigrette. Arrange lettuce leaves on a serving plate and chicken, fruit, and nuts in the center. *Serves 4 as main course.*

INGREDIENTS:
2 whole chicken breasts, cooked
2 tart, ripe, unpeeled apples such as Granny Smiths, cored and cut in thin slices
1 cup small seedless green or red grapes
½ cup chopped walnuts
Red or green lettuce leaves

VINAIGRETTE:
⅓ cup extra-virgin olive oil
¼ cup raspberry vinegar
salt and freshly ground black pepper to taste

EQUIPMENT:
Small bowl or 2-cup measuring cup
Medium (2 ½ quart) mixing bowl

TIPS: Poach chicken with skin on the bone for bet-better flavor. After cooking, remove skin and bone. Toast walnuts lightly in a 300° oven for about 10 minutes. Cool before using.

Appetizers

Hearty Mediterranean Soup

This soup is so full of flavor it doesn't require a meat- or vegetable-broth base, but if you prefer one, substitute full-strength or diluted broth for the water.

INGREDIENTS:
- 3 tablespoons olive oil
- 3 leeks, white parts and 1 inch of the green, sliced
- 2 red onions, thinly sliced
- 3 garlic cloves, minced
- 1½ to 2 quarts water
- 1 head red cabbage, cored and finely shredded
- 1 (8-ounce) can fava beans (or white beans)
- 1 teaspoon dried rosemary
- 8 to 10 cups shredded spinach leaves
- Salt and freshly ground black pepper to taste
- Toasted garlic bread with Parmesan cheese for garnish (optional)

EQUIPMENT:
- 4½-quart covered Dutch oven

> **TIP:** To eliminate fat entirely, skip the sauteing step and add the leeks, onions, and garlic directly to boiling water.

Heat oil in Dutch oven over medium heat; add leeks, onions, and garlic and saute briefly. Add water, cabbage, beans, and rosemary. Bring to a boil, cover, and simmer ½ hour; remove lid and simmer 1 more hour. Add spinach 5 minutes before serving. You can garnish the soup with toasted garlic bread and Parmesan cheese. To prepare: Toast bread and spread with olive oil and some finely minced garlic. Sprinkle with grated Parmesan cheese and float the toast in individual soup bowls. Spoon hot soup over the bread to melt the cheese and soften the toast. *Serves 6.*

Potato-Plus Soup

INGREDIENTS:
2 quarts water
1 large red potato, unpeeled
1 medium Idaho potato, peeled
1 medium yam, peeled
2 carrots, scrubbed well or peeled
1 large onion, peeled
2 turnips, peeled
2 parsnips, peeled
2 stalks celery, including leaves
1 tablespoon fresh rosemary leaves or dill or
1 teaspoon dried ground cardamom
Salt and freshly ground black pepper to taste
Plain yogurt or sour cream for garnish (optional)
Fresh chopped parsley for garnish

EQUIPMENT:
4 1/2-quart covered Dutch oven or stockpot

Bring water to a boil. Cut all vegetables into small dice; add to boiling water. Add herbs and seasoning to taste; reduce heat and simmer, covered, 4 hours or more, adding water as necessary. Garnish each serving as desired. *Serves 6.*

III. POULTRY

Japanese Chicken, Carrots, and Parsnips

Try this healthy, delicately flavored dish served over rice.

INGREDIENTS:
- 2 whole chicken breasts, rinsed, skinned, boned, and cut into bite-sized pieces
- ¼ cup soy sauce
- 12 baby carrots, scrubbed and quartered
- 6 young parsnips, peeled and sliced in thin rounds
- 1 tablespoon grated fresh ginger
- 2 teaspoons vegetable or peanut oil
- 1 tablespoon white or rice vinegar
- Pinch of sugar
- 2 to 3 scallions for garnish, white and tender greens, sliced lengthwise

EQUIPMENT:
- Glass pie plate
- 3-quart covered double boiler
- Small bowl or 2-cup measuring cup

Place chicken and soy sauce in pie plate, mix to coat and marinate 15 minutes, stirring occasionally. Put chicken with sauce in top of double boiler. Add carrots and parsnips. Cover with ginger. Mix together oil, vinegar, and sugar; drizzle over chicken and vegetables. Cover and cook 10 to 15 minutes over boiling water. Garnish with fresh scallions. *Serves 6*

Roast Turkey

Turkey is one of the leanest types of poultry. The exception to that is the self-basting variety, which is injected with butter or corn, soybean, or coconut oil.

Preheat oven to 450°. Remove giblets and reserve if making stock (see below). Rinse turkey well inside and out. Pat dry and put about 6 cups stuffing into turkey cavity and another 2 cups stuffing in neck area. Fill the cavity and neck only ¾ full to allow room for the stuffing to swell as it cooks. Note: Never stuff a turkey until you're ready to roast it; a stuffed turkey is a breeding ground for bacteria. Close cavity opening with small skewers and a crisscrossed string. Secure neck flap under turkey. Fasten legs close to body with string. Rub skin with butter and place bird, breast side up, on rack in uncovered roasting pan. Reduce oven heat to 325°, and roast according to directions below. After 30 minutes begin basting turkey with pan drippings, chicken broth, or butter, at least once every hour. Let turkey stand a minimum of 15 minutes before carving.

To make gravy, pour off and strain pan juices into a saucepan. Remove fat by tipping pan and skimming off fat with a spoon. Add giblet stock, canned chicken stock, or water until you have about 3½ cups. Heat to a simmer. In small bowl, stir flour into ¼ cup water; add to saucepan a little at a time, stirring constantly with a whisk until well blended. Heat to a boil and simmer 5 minutes. Salt and pepper to taste. *Serves 8 to 10.*

INGREDIENTS:
1 fresh turkey, about 15 pounds
8 cups stuffing of your choice (see p.52-53)
Unsalted butter
For the gravy:
3½ cups liquid, either giblet stock, canned chicken stock, or water
¼ cup flour
½ cup water
Salt and freshly ground black pepper to taste

EQUIPMENT:
Deep roasting pan with rack
2-quart saucepan
Small bowl or 2-cup measuring cup

COOKING TIMES: Allow 15 to 20 minutes per pound; for a turkey over 16 pounds, allow 13 to 15 minutes per pound. Add 5 minutes per pound for a stuffed turkey. For more accurate timing, insert a thermometer in center of inner thigh and cook until it reaches 185°. Prick the skin of the thigh to see if the juice runs clear.

POULTRY

TIP: Giblet stock can be made by simmering giblets with 1 whole onion and 1 scrubbed carrot in 4 cups water for 1 hour; discard vegetables and giblets, and strain.

Wild-Rice Stuffing a L'Orange

Bring salted water to a boil in saucepan. Add giblets and necks, reduce heat, and simmer about 20 minutes. Remove giblets, chop, and reserve; discard necks. Raise heat to high, bring stock to a rolling boil, and add wild rice. Lower heat immediately, cover, and simmer, stirring occasionally, 30 minutes, or until rice is almost tender and most of the stock is absorbed.

Melt butter in sauté pan and sauté shallots and green pepper 3 minutes. Remove from heat. Add chopped giblets, grated orange rind, drained rice, salt, and pepper to the shallots and green pepper in the pan, mixing well. *Yield: about 3 cups.*

INGREDIENTS:
Giblets and necks of game hens or chicken, rinsed
4 cups water
Pinch of salt
1 cup wild rice
4 tablespoons butter or margarine
3 shallots, minced
1 tablespoon finely chopped green bell pepper
1 tablespoon of finely grated orange rind
Salt and freshly ground pepper to taste

EQUIPMENT:
2 ½ quart covered saucepan
10-inch saute pan

Fresh Cranberry-Orange Relish

Put half the cranberries and half of the orange sections into the container of a food processor; process until mixture is coarsely chopped with no whole berries remaining. Transfer to a storage container and process the remaining cranberries and orange sections. Combine the two mixtures and stir in sugar to taste. Refrigerate, ideally for several days before serving, to allow flavors to blend. *Yield: about 2½ cups.*

INGREDIENTS:
12 ounces fresh cranberries, rinsed and picked over to remove stems
1 medium seedless orange, cut into eighths, do not peel
½ to ¾ cup sugar
½ teaspoon chopped fresh ginger (optional)

EQUIPMENT:
Food processor or blender
Refrigerator storage container

Curried Chicken-Broccoli Casserole

Serve over rice to catch the sauce and make a complete meal.

> INGREDIENTS:
> 1½ pounds, 1 large bunch, fresh broccoli, broken into six to eight stalks
> 2 tablespoons butter or margarine
> 2 tablespoons vegetable oil
> 3 whole chicken breasts, rinsed, skinned, and cut in half
> Salt and freshly ground black pepper to taste.
> 1 recipe Bechamel Sauce (see p. 124)
> 3 tablespoons curry powder
> 3 tablespoons light cream
> Generous squeeze fresh lemon (optional)
>
> EQUIPMENT:
> 2-quart covered saucepan with steamer
> 3-quart covered casserole
> 1-quart saucepan

Cook broccoli for 5 minutes in steamer. Preheat oven to 350°. In casserole over medium-high heat, cook butter and oil until it foams. Place chicken breasts in one layer and brown 2 to 3 minutes on each side. Remove chicken; drain off all fat and wipe pan with a paper towel.

In small saucepan, prepare Bechamel Sauce — or reheat previously prepared sauce, adding curry powder during last few minutes of cooking. Add cream one tablespoon at a time, blending well, and a squeeze of lemon. Put broccoli in casserole, add chicken and sprinkle with salt and pepper. Pour sauce over chicken and broccoli and bake covered 15 minutes. Remove lid and bake 10 to 15 more minutes until chicken is cooked through. Serve over rice. *Serves 6.*

> TIP: To reduce fat, poach the chicken instead of browning it in butter and oil.

IV. Fish

Hot Snapper Veracruz

Serve this spicy snapper over white rice to absorb the delicious juices. Cool down with Minted Cucumber Salad (see p. 10) and a classically simple steamed or sautéed zucchini dish.

INGREDIENTS:
- 4 red snapper fillets, about 6 ounces each
- Juice of 3 to 4 limes
- 3 tablespoons olive oil
- 2 garlic cloves, minced
- 1 onion, chopped
- 3 to 4 small tomatoes, chopped
- 1 or 2 jalapeño peppers, seeded and finely chopped
- Salt and freshly ground black pepper to taste
- 1/3 cup chopped fresh cilantro leaves

EQUIPMENT:
- 9 x 13-inch baking dish
- 8-inch sauté pan

Place fish in greased baking dish. Add lime juice to nearly cover and marinate 30 minutes, turning fillets once. In sauté pan, heat oil over medium high heat; add garlic and onion and sauté 3 to 4 minutes. Add tomatoes and jalapeños and simmer gently 5 minutes. Preheat oven to 350°. Spread tomato sauce over fish (leave lime-juice marinade in pan) and sprinkle with cilantro. Cover and bake 20 minutes or until fish flakes with a fork. *Serves 4.*

TIP: To avoid contact with skin, wear rubber gloves when preparing jalapeños.

Fillet of Sole with Tomatoes and Parsley

Preheat oven to 350°. Heat olive oil in saute pan and saute tomatoes, onion, and garlic for 10 minutes, or until wilted. Add wine and cook to reduce by one half. Stir in lemon juice. Arrange fillets in a layer in greased baking dish. Pour tomato mixture over fish, sprinkle with parsley, oregano, salt, and pepper. Bake 12 to 15 minutes or until fish flakes with a fork. Serve with rice. *Serves 4.*

INGREDIENTS:
1 tablespoon olive oil
4 medium tomatoes, chopped
1 small onion, chopped
1 garlic clove, minced
½ cup dry white wine
2 tablespoons fresh lemon juice
4 fillets of sole, about 6 ounces each
¼ cup minced Italian flat-leaf parsley
¼ teaspoon dried oregano
Salt and freshly ground black pepper to taste

EQUIPMENT
10-inch sauté pan
4-quart (15 x 10 x 2-inch) baking dish or casserole

FISH

Halibut with Confetti Sauce

INGREDIENTS:
4 halibut steaks, about 6 ounces each
½ cup fresh lemon juice
Salt and freshly ground black or white pepper to taste
¼ cup chopped scallions, white and tender greens
2 cups shredded carrots
¼ cup chopped fresh Italian flat-leaf parsley
3 tablespoons chopped fresh dill
2 large tomatoes, peeled and chopped
½ cup bean sprouts or julienned cucumber
1 lemon, cut in wedges

EQUIPMENT:
4-quart covered casserole or 15 x 10 x 2-inch baking dish
Medium (2 ½-quart) mixing bowl

Preheat oven to 350°. Place halibut in baking dish and season with lemon juice, salt, and pepper. In bowl, toss together scallions, carrots, parsley, and dill and spoon over fish. Cover and bake 20 minutes or until fish flakes with a fork. Garnish with chopped tomato, bean sprouts or cucumber, and lemon wedges. *Serves 4.*

25

Creamy Non-Dairy Pimento Sauce

This sauce is simple to prepare and terrific over fish.

INGREDIENTS:
- 1 (12-ounce) container soft tofu, drained
- 1 (6-ounce) can whole pimentos, drained
- 1 teaspoon or more ground cumin
- 1 teaspoon or more paprika
- 1 to 2 garlic cloves, peeled
- 2 tablespoons cider vinegar
- 1 tablespoon olive oil
- 2 tablespoons Worcestershire sauce
- 2 tablespoons capers, drained
- 1 tablespoon fresh lemon juice
- 6 to 8 small sun-dried tomatoes, reconstituted in boiling water for 3 minutes and drained
- ¼ cup toasted almonds (optional)

EQUIPMENT:
Food processor or blender
2-quart saucepan

Place all ingredients in food processor and blend until very smooth. Allow to stand 1 hour to blend flavors. Taste and correct seasoning, then heat in a saucepan over medium-low heat. *Yield: about 3 cups.*

V. Meat

Grilled Lamb Kebabs

INGREDIENTS:
½ Cup olive oil
Juice of 1 lemon and grated zest
1 garlic clove, minced
1 tablespoon fresh rosemary sprigs or 1½ teaspoons dried rosemary
1 tablespoon ground coriander
1 teaspoon salt
Several grinds of black pepper
2 pounds lamb, cut into 2-inch cubes

EQUIPMENT:
Large (4-quart) mixing bowl
Skewers

TIPS: Large cherry tomatoes, onion, and bell-pepper wedges can be skewered between lamb chunks Brush with marinade.

To broil kebabs in the oven, preheat oven to Broil and follow instructions above.

If you use wooden skewers soak them in water for about an hour before threading meat; otherwise they may ignite.

Mix first 7 ingredients in bowl. Add lamb and marinate in refrigerator 8 hours or overnight, turning occasionally. Drain lamb and place on skewers. Reserve marinade. Grill over hot coals basting occasionally with marinade: 5 minutes on each side for medium rare; 7 minutes on each side for medium. *Serves 4 to 6.*

27

Roast Leg of Spring Lamb with Fresh Mint Vinaigrette

For delicious lamb *do not over cook*. The roast is at its juicy, succulent best when served rare or medium rare.

INGREDIENTS:
1 leg of spring lamb, 6 to 7 pounds, trimmed of all excess fat
2 garlic cloves, sliced into about 6 slivers each
3 tablespoons extra-virgin olive oil
Salt and freshly ground black pepper to taste
1 or more cups dry white wine

VINAIGRETTE:
2/3 cup olive oil
1/4 cup white wine vinegar
1 teaspoon sugar
Salt and freshly ground black pepper to taste
3/4 cup finely chopped fresh mint leaves

EQUIPMENT:
Deep roasting pan with rack
Small (1-quart) mixing bowl

With the point of a sharp knife, pierce lamb in as many places as you have garlic slivers. Insert slivers into slits. Refrigerate lamb 2 hours, the remove from refrigerator and let stand at room temperature 30 minutes.

Preheat oven to 325°. Rub leg of lamb all over with oil, sprinkle with salt and pepper, place on rack in roasting pan, and pour 1 cup of the wine around it. Insert meat thermometer in thickest part of meat away from bone and roast 20 minutes per pound for rare (135 to 140° degrees internal temperature) or 25 minutes per pound for medium (150 to 155° internal temperature). Baste occasionally with wine and any juices that accumulate, adding more wine if necessary.

To make vinaigrette, place all ingredients except mint in bowl and whisk until sugar completely dissolves. Add mint and mix well. Cover bowl and let it sit about 30 minutes to allow flavors to blend. Immediately before serving whisk again.

Transfer lamb to heated platter and let stand about 15 min-utes. Slice thinly and serve with vinaigrette. *Serves 8.*

> **TIP:** To shorten cooking time, have the butcher bone and tie leg of lamb. Insert garlic slivers and marinate as indicated above. Preheat oven to 425°. Sear lamb on all sides over high heat in ovenproof skillet; transfer to oven and roast without basting 25 to 30 minutes then proceed with recipe.

Baja Tacos

INGREDIENTS:
1 package corn tortillas, preferably blue corn
1 pound lean ground beef
2 tablespoons red-wine vinegar
4 to 6 scallions, white and tender greens, chopped
1 teaspoon ground cumin
2 tablespoons chili powder
1 (8-ounce) can tomato sauce
2 drops hot pepper sauce

Salt and cayenne pepper to taste

TOPPINGS:
Chopped tomatoes, salsa, grated cheddar cheese, avocado slices, sour cream, chopped fresh cilantro leaves, fresh watercress or arugula

EQUIPMENT:
10-inch skillet

Preheat oven to 350°. Wrap tortillas in aluminum foil and warm in oven while meal is prepared. Heat skillet over medium-high heat, add beef, and brown. Drain fat and add remaining ingredients. Stir and cook 15 to 20 minutes over medium heat. Serve with tortillas and generous amounts of toppings on the side; let everyone assemble his or her own tacos. *Serves 4.*

TIP: You can also blend the cooked beef with chopped tomato and/or salsa "garnish" to simplify the assembly of tacos.

Peppers and Steak

Serve on lettuce boats, Boston or bibb lettuce; flour tortillas, or crusty sandwich rolls.

> INGREDIENTS:
> 4 tablespoons olive oil
> 2 shallots, sliced
> 2 small red, green, or yellow bell peppers, seeded, cored, and sliced
> 2 to 3 cherry peppers or equivalent amount of hot pepper, seeded and sliced
> 1 garlic clove, mashed
> 2 tablespoons red-wine vinegar
> 2 to 3 skirt steaks, about 4 to 5 ounces each
> Salt and freshly ground black pepper to taste
>
> EQUIPMENT:
> 10-inch skillet

Heat 3 tablespoons oil in skillet over medium-high heat. Add shallots, peppers, garlic, and vinegar. Sauté 10 minutes. Remove peppers, from skillet; drain if necessary and set aside in warm oven. Drain skillet and wipe clean. Heat remaining tablespoon of olive oil in skillet over high heat. Add steaks, cooking about 3 minutes on each side; they will still be red in the center. Remove steaks and slice at an angle across the grain into thin strips. Combine with peppers and season with salt and pepper. *Serves 4.*

MEAT

VI. Vegetables

Broccoli, Carrot, and Spinach Timbales

INGREDIENTS:
1 pound carrots, peeled and sliced in discs
1 pound broccoli, trimmed and cut into stems with florets
4 eggs
2 tablespoons light cream
Salt and freshly ground black pepper to taste
½ teaspoon dried ground cardamom
½ teaspoon dried ground mace
5 tablespoons butter or margarine
8 cups fresh spinach

EQUIPMENT:
2 2-quart covered saucepans with steamers
Food processor or blender
Small (1-quart) mixing bowl
6 ½-cup timbale molds or ramekins
Large baking pan

Preheat oven to 350°. Steam carrots and broccoli in separate pans for 15 minutes or until very soft. Puree each vegetable separately in food processor. In bowl, whisk together eggs and cream; divide mixture in half and blend with pureed vegetables in separate pans. Add cardamom to carrots and mace to broccoli; add 2 tablespoons of butter to each and cook over low heat for just a minute. Place broccoli puree in greased ramekins: top with carrot puree. Place ramekins in bain-marie, a large baking pan with hot water that reaches halfway up the ramekins, and bake 20 to 25 minutes or until a toothpick inserted in the center comes out clean. When timbales are nearly done, thoroughly wash spinach and place in saucepan with water still clinging to leaves. Cover and cook over low heat for 2 to 3 minutes. Serve unmolded timbales on a bed of spinach. *Serves 6.*

VEGETABLES

TIP: If you don't have mace and cardamom on hand, season the timbales with nutmeg. To save time, microwave the vegetables.

Corn Pudding

Wonderful with grilled meats, chops, sausage. Fresh summer corn needs no extra seasoning.

INGREDIENTS:
2 eggs, separated
6 ears corn, grated
1 tablespoon melted butter or margarine
1 tablespoon sugar
½ cup milk
½ teaspoon baking powder
Salt and freshly ground black pepper to taste
Pinch of nutmeg (optional)

EQUIPMENT:
2 medium (2 ½ quart) mixing bowls
2 ½-quart casserole or souffle dish
Electric mixer

TIP: Corn must be grated. You can use frozen corn-on-the-cob, but not frozen kernels.

Preheat oven to 350°. Beat egg yolks lightly and egg whites until stiff. Mix all ingredients except egg whites. Fold in beaten egg whites and pour into baking dish. Bake 30 minutes or until knife inserted in center comes out clean. *Serves 4 to 6.*

New Cottage Potatoes

INGREDIENTS:
12 to 16 small new potatoes
½ cup cottage cheese
Salt and paprika to taste

EQUIPMENT:
3-quart saucepan

Bring water to boil in saucepan. Add potatoes and boil, uncovered, for 10 to 15 minutes or until tender. Drain and place in serving bowl. Mash potatoes with large fork, add cottage cheese, salt, and paprika. Blend with fork and serve. Mixture should be chunky, not smooth. *Serves 4.*

Steamed Zucchini with Tomatoes

While beef is cooking, prepare this steamed-vegetable dish.

INGREDIENTS:
3 small zucchini, thinly sliced
1 pint cherry tomatoes, stems removed
1 tablespoon olive oil
1 to 2 teaspoons dried marjoram
Salt and freshly ground black pepper to taste

EQUIPMENT:
2-quart covered saucepan with steamer

Bring water to a boil in saucepan, place zucchini in steamer and steam for 3 to 4 minutes until tender-crisp. Add tomatoes and steam for an additional minute or until tomatoes are warm. Remove to a serving bowl; toss with olive oil and marjoram, salt and pepper. *Serves 4.*

Baked Tomatoes Provençale

INGREDIENTS
2 garlic cloves, minced
1 shallot, minced
2 tablespoons finely chopped fresh Italian flat-leaf parsley
2 tablespoons finely chopped fresh basil leaves
1 teaspoon finely chopped fresh thyme leaves
Salt and coarsely ground black pepper to taste
3 tablespoons, plus 1 teaspoon olive oil
4 large, ripe tomatoes, cut in half crosswise

EQUIPMENT:
Small (1-quart) mixing bowl
9 x 13-inch baking dish

Preheat oven to 425°. Place garlic, shallot, herbs, salt and pepper, and 3 tablespoons of the oil in bowl and mash to a coarse paste with the back of a wooden spoon. Grease baking dish with remaining oil. Place tomato halves in dish, cut-side up, and spread with herb mixture. Bake 10 minutes, or until topping begins to bubble. Serve hot or at room temperature. *Serves 4.*

VEGETABLES

Winter Vegetable Potpourri

INGREDIENTS:
1 large Idaho potato, peeled
2 medium white turnips, peeled and stem end trimmed
12 baby carrots, peeled, or 6 medium carrots, peeled and cut in 1-inch-thick rounds
12 small white onions, peeled
¼ pound green beans, cut into 2-inch pieces
3 tablespoons butter or margarine
1 shallot, finely chopped
Salt and freshly ground black pepper to taste
1½ teaspoons fresh thyme leaves or ½ teaspoon dried thyme

EQUIPMENT:
3 quart saucepan
10-inch sauté pan

Cut potato and turnips in half, then slice halves into 6 or 8 pieces. Place carrots and onions in saucepan. Add water to cover and a pinch of salt. Bring to a boil over medium heat, then lower heat and simmer 5 minutes. Add turnips and potato and cook 5 minutes. Add green beans; cook 5 more minutes until just tender. Drain and set aside.

Heat butter in sauté pan over medium heat until bubbling but not brown. Add shallots and cook 2 to 3 minutes. Add drained vegetables, salt, pepper, and thyme. Cook 2 minutes, stirring constantly. *Serves 4.*

TIP: To peel small white onions: Drop into boiling water; boil 1 minute; drain under cold running water; trim off both ends; slip of skins.

VEGETABLES

Red Onion Preserves

Serve as a condiment with ground beef dishes—or serve on the side with beef, poultry, or fish.

INGREDIENTS:
- 1/4 cup olive oil
- 1 tablespoon minced garlic
- 1/2 teaspoon ground cumin
- 1/2 teaspoon red pepper flakes
- 1 teaspoon dried oregano
- 1 bay leaf
- 1/4 cup balsamic vinegar
- Salt to taste
- 1 teaspoon coarsely ground black pepper
- 3 pounds red onions, cut in 1/2-inch slices

EQUIPMENT:
- 12-inch covered sauté pan or sautôir

Heat oil in sauté pan over medium-high heat. Add garlic and sauté 1 minute. Add remaining ingredients, except onions, and stir. Add onion, stir, and reduce heat to low. Cover and cook about 45 minutes to 1 hour until onion is very soft, stirring several times. Do not allow to burn. Let cool to room temperature and refrigerate at least 1 day. To serve, remove bay leaf and let preserves return to room temperature. *Yield: about 2 cups.*

MICROWAVE DIRECTIONS: Combine all ingredients except salt, pepper, and vinegar in shallow microwave dish. Loosely cover with glass cover (or microwavable plastic wrap, but make sure it doesn't touch food.) Cook on HIGH 4 minutes. Stir; cook on HIGH an additional 4 minutes. Add vinegar; continue cooking, uncovered, on HIGH 4 minutes. Add salt and pepper.

VEGETABLES

VII. Beans/Rice/Pasta

Frutta di Mare Pasta

Examine mussels, discard any that are cracked or not tightly closed. Scrub mussels thoroughly under running water, pulling out and discarding fiber-like "beards" from between shells. Scrub clams and place in cold water to cover until ready to use.

Heat oil in stockpot over medium-heat, add garlic, and sauté just 1 minute. Add wine and simmer 1 more minute. Add all remaining ingredients, including ½ cup reserved tomato juice, except shellfish and pasta. Bring to a boil, then reduce heat and simmer 5 minutes.

Add clams and mussels to sauce, cover tightly and cook 5 minutes. Add scallops and shrimp and cook covered 5 to 10 minutes more, or until clams and mussels open, scallops are opaque, and shrimp are pink. Do not over cook or shellfish will become tough. Serve over fettuccine or spaghetti, cooked according to package directions. *Serves 8.*

INGREDIENTS:
2 pounds large mussels
8 cherrystone clams
6 tablespoons extra-virgin olive oil
4 garlic cloves, finely minced
½ cup dry white wine
2 cups canned whole Italian tomatoes, drained but reserving ½ cup juice
1 tablespoon tomato paste
Salt and freshly ground black pepper to taste
½ cup finely chopped Italian flat-leaf parsley
1 pound bay or sea scallops
1 pound medium shrimp, shelled and deveined
1½ pounds fettuccine or spaghetti

EQUIPMENT:
2 8-quart stockpots, 1 covered

Beans/Rice/Pasta

Presto Pizza

A no-yeast pizza dough that's ready to bake in less than 10 minutes. For appetizers, instead of making one large pizza, cut the dough into small circles with a cookie cutter.

INGREDIENTS
2 ¼ cups all-purpose flour
1½ tablespoons baking powder
1 teaspoon salt
8 tablespoons olive oil
⅓ cup water

EQUIPMENT:
Large (4-quart) mixing bowl
12- to 14-inch pizza pan or baking sheet

SUGGESTED TOPPINGS

PIZZA CLASSICO: Grated fresh mozzarella cheese, Thick and Hearty Tomato Sauce (see p. 123), slivered green bell peppers, freshly grated Parmesan or Romano cheese, dried oregano or marjoram, and olive oil. Cover with tomato sauce, sprinkle with mozzarella, add pepper slivers, sprinkle with Parmesan or Romano cheese and herbs. Drizzle lightly with olive oil; bake 15 minutes.

ARTICHOKE PIZZA: Slices of fresh mozzarella cheese, Red Pepper Sauce (see p. 124), sautéed or steamed artichoke hearts, sliced, and olive oil. Cover pizza with sauce, arrange slices of mozzarella and artichoke hearts on top, drizzle with olive oil; bake 15 minutes.

PIZZA ALLA PESTO: Steamed spinach, grated parmesan or Romano cheese, Pesto Sauce (see p. 123). After brushing pizza with olive oil, bake for 10 minutes or until golden. Remove from oven, spread with half of the pesto, cover with spinach, sprinkle with grated cheese, and "dot" with remaining pesto. Return to oven and bake 2 to 3 more minutes.

PIZZA FRESCO: Chopped fresh tomatoes, chopped fresh basil leaves, salt and pepper to taste, and fresh mozzarella slices. Cover pizza with chopped tomatoes, sprinkle with basil, season with salt and pepper, and cover with mozzarella slices; bake 15 minutes.

Preheat oven to 450°. Sift dry ingredients into bowl. Add water and 6 tablespoons oil; mix with your hands until ingredients form a soft dough. Put dough on lightly floured surface and knead gently about 30 seconds. Press or roll dough into a flat circle about ⅛-inch thick. Turn up edges to make a rim, place on ungreased pizza pan, and brush with remaining 2 tablespoons olive oil. Let stand 5 minutes. Add toppings of choice and bake as indicated below. *Yield: 1 pizza.*

Beans/Rice/Pasta

Angel-Hair Pasta and Artichokes

INGREDIENTS:
1 pound angel-hair pasta
2 (10-ounce) packages frozen artichoke hearts, thawed
4 tablespoons olive oil
¼ cup grated Parmesan cheese
2 tablespoons chopped fresh marjoram leaves or 2 teaspoons dried marjoram
2 garlic cloves, quartered
¼ cup sliced scallions, white and tender greens
1 generous squeeze fresh lemon juice
Salt and freshly ground black pepper to taste

EQUIPMENT:
6-quart stockpot
Food processor or blender
10-inch sauté pan

Prepare pasta in stockpot according to package directions. In food processor, puree thoroughly two-thirds of the artichokes, 3 tablespoons of the oil, Parmesan cheese, marjoram, garlic, and scallions. Coarsely chop remaining artichokes and squeeze lemon juice over them. Heat remaining tablespoon of oil in sauté pan over medium-high heat; add chopped artichokes and saute 6 to 8 minutes or until tender. Add artichoke puree to pan and cook over medium heat until heated through. Season with salt and pepper to taste. Toss with pasta. *Serves 4.*

BEANS/RICE/PASTA

Red Pepper Sauce

This sauce is velvety smooth and wonderful over ravioli or angel-hair pasta. It's also a nice addition to lasagna, pizza, and many vegetable dishes that require tomato sauce. Freeze it in small quantities so that it's always on hand. Use it sparingly, though, because it has a more intense flavor than a tomato sauce.

INGREDIENTS:
3 tablespoons olive oil
1 garlic clove, minced
6 red bell peppers, roasted (see p.)
2 teaspoons balsamic vinegar
Salt and freshly ground black pepper to taste

EQUIPMENT:
8-inch sauté pan
Food processor or blender

In sauté pan, heat 1 tablespoon of the oil over medium-high heat. Add garlic and cook 1 to 2 minutes. Do not brown. Place roasted peppers in food processor with sautéed garlic, remaining olive oil and vinegar; process until finely blended. Serve at room temperature over pasta or reheat briefly. *Yield: about 3 cups.*

TIP: Roasted peppers covered with a little olive oil should keep for at least a week in your refrigerator.

VARIATION: Crushed tomatoes can be substituted for some of the peppers. Use 3 to 4 peppers and 1 cup crushed tomatoes.

Beans/Rice/Pasta

Pumpkin Bread

INGREDIENTS:
¼ cup vegetable oil
¼ cup melted butter or margarine
¾ cup sugar
1 egg
1 cup pumpkin puree (not pumpkin-pie filling), canned
1 cup grated, unpeeled apple
2 cups all-purpose flour
1 teaspoon baking soda
½ teaspoon baking powder
¼ teaspoon salt
½ teaspoon cinnamon
¼ cup sesame seeds or chopped nuts (optional)
½ cup raisins (optional)

TOPPING
2 tablespoons butter
2 tablespoons sugar
2 tablespoons flour
½ teaspoon cinnamon

EQUIPMENT:
Large (4-quart) mixing bowl
2 small (1-quart) mixing bowls
1½-quart loaf pan

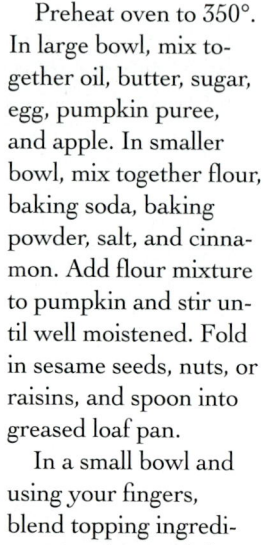

Preheat oven to 350°. In large bowl, mix together oil, butter, sugar, egg, pumpkin puree, and apple. In smaller bowl, mix together flour, baking soda, baking powder, salt, and cinnamon. Add flour mixture to pumpkin and stir until well moistened. Fold in sesame seeds, nuts, or raisins, and spoon into greased loaf pan.

In a small bowl and using your fingers, blend topping ingredients together until they form a coarse meal. Sprinkle on top of loaf. Bake 40 minutes or until toothpick inserted in center comes out clean. Remove from pan and cool on rack. *Yield: 1 loaf.*

Italian Bread with Olive Oil and Herbs

Healthier than buttered garlic bread and just as delicious.

INGREDIENTS:
½ cup extra-virgin olive oil
1 teaspoon mixed dried herbs, oregano, marjoram, and thyme
Pinch of salt
1 loaf Italian bread
Grated Parmesan cheese (optional)

EQUIPMENT:
Small bowl or 2-cup measuring cup
Baking sheet

Preheat oven to Broil. Whisk olive oil, herbs and salt in bowl until thoroughly blended. Slice bread in half lengthwise, and drizzle olive-oil mixture over both cut surfaces. (If loaf is exceptionally large, you may need to increase quantities of oil and herbs.) Place bread on baking sheet; broil, cut-sides up, for 1 to 2 minutes or until surface of bread is lightly browned. Serve warm. Sprinkle with cheese if desired. *Serves 6*

Banana-Fig Bread

INGREDIENTS:
1¾ cups all-purpose flour
1 tablespoon baking powder
½ cup sugar
⅓ cup butter or margarine
2 eggs
3 medium bananas, about 1 cup, mashed
1 teaspoon grated orange rind
¼ cup finely chopped dried figs

EQUIPMENT:
Large (4-quart) mixing bowl
Small (1½-quart) mixing bowl
1½-quart loaf pan

Preheat oven to 350°. Into large bowl sift together flour and baking powder. In small bowl beat sugar and butter together until creamy. Add egg mixture to dry ingredients. Stir just until smooth. Add bananas, orange rind, and figs; stir again. Pour into greased loaf pan. Bake 45 minutes or until firmly set when lightly touched on center top. Cool on rack. Remove from pan after 10 minutes. *Yield: 1 loaf.*

TIP: Toss figs with sugar or some flour to make them easier to chop.

Beans/Rice/Pasta

VIII. Desserts

Chocolate Angel-Food Cake

This low-fat, low-cholesterol dessert is a perennial favorite. There is no fat at all if you make a plain angel-food cake by replacing the ¼ cup cocoa in this recipe with an additional ¼ cup cake flour.

INGREDIENTS:
1½ cups egg whites (about 10 eggs) at room temperature
1¼ teaspoons cream of tartar
¼ teaspoon salt
1 teaspoon vanilla extract
1¼ cups sugar
¾ cups cake flour
¼ cup cocoa

EQUIPMENT:
Large (4-quart) mixing bowl
Electric mixer
Small (1-quart) mixing bowl
10-inch nonstick tube pan

TIP: Because egg sizes vary significantly, add egg whites one at a time to measuring cup.

Combine egg whites, cream of tartar, salt, vanilla in large bowl and beat with electric mixer until mixture holds peaks. Continue beating adding ½ cup of the sugar a little at a time. In a bowl, blend flour, cocoa, and remaining sugar mixture on top of egg whites and gently fold in with a rubber spatula.

Spoon batter into tube pan and bake 30 minutes or until a toothpick inserted in cake comes out clean. Remove from oven, immediately turn pan upside down on rack, but do not remove cake. When cool, remove cake and serve pieces with a melted chocolate glaze. *Serves 6.*

Raspberry Sauce

Try this sauce over ice cream, fresh peaches, pound cake, pears, or Chocolate Torte (see p. 56).

INGREDIENTS:
1 (10-ounce) package frozen raspberries in light syrup
1 teaspoon grated lemon rind
½ cup raspberry jam or currant jelly
1½ teaspoons cornstarch
1 tablespoon fresh lemon juice
EQUIPMENT:
1-quart measuring cup
Sieve
Small dish

Place raspberries in a nonreactive saucepan or microwave dish, breaking up raspberries occasionally as they thaw. Stir in lemon rind and jam. Bring to a boil or heat in microwave oven 3 to 5 minutes on HIGH, stirring at 1-minute intervals.

Strain mixture through a sieve to remove seeds and rind. Return mixture to saucepan or dish.

Mix cornstarch and lemon juice in a small dish and add to raspberries. Cook on low heat, stirring until mixture clears. Cool by refrigerating immediately in the same cooking pan. Stir frequently during cooling. *Yield: about 1 cup.*

Chocolate Torte

This delicious dessert tastes somewhat like a brownie—but better. Because there is no flour, it is very moist and dense without feeling heavy. For chocolate lovers, this torte is sheer perfection.

INGREDIENTS:
5 ounces semisweet chocolate
10 tablespoons butter (we don't recommend margarine)
2/3 cup sugar
5 eggs, separated

EQUIPMENT:
1-quart saucepan
Large (4-quart) mixing bowl
Electric mixer
Medium (2 1/2-quart) mixing bowl
9-inch round cake pan

TIP: Make sure the beaters are completely fat-free before beating egg whites. Even a drop of chocolate or egg yolk can prevent the whites from becoming stiff.

Preheat oven to 325°. Melt chocolate and butter together in saucepan over low heat, stirring occasionally. Remove saucepan from heat, add sugar and mix thoroughly, and allow to cool. Place egg yolks in large bowl, add chocolate mixture, and beat 10 to 15 minutes with electric mixer on high. In medium bowl, beat egg whites until stiff and gently fold into chocolate mixture with a spatula. Pour batter into well-greased and floured 9-inch cake pan. Bake 35 minutes or until torte rises and top is firm. It will still seem moist in center so a toothpick inserted into center won't be clean; it should still have some chocolate clinging to it.

Let torte cool in pan for 8 to 10 minutes; it will fall slightly. To remove from pan, carefully run a thin knife around the edge. Hold cake rack on top of pan and flip over; gently lift pan from torte. Holding a serving plate against torte, quickly flip over again so that the "rounded" side of torte is up. Allow torte to cool thoroughly before serving. It can be refrigerated for several days but return to room temperature before serving. Serve plain or sprinkle with confectioner's sugar—or decorate with fresh raspberries, candied orange peel, or chocolate shavings.
Serves 6

DESSERTS

Iced Winter Fruit

An elegantly simple dessert, perfect for a party.

INGREDIENTS:
2 to 3 large bunches of red grapes
About ¼ cup superfine sugar
4 tangerines or oranges, peeled and in segments
8 ounces bittersweet chocolate

EQUIPMENT:
Freezer storage container
Double boiler
Baking sheet

Leaving them in bunches, wash grapes. While still wet, sprinkle with sugar. Put in a freezer storage container and freeze at least 2 hours.

Melt the chocolate in double boiler over hot (not simmering) water. Use a toothpick to dip the orange segments in the chocolate. Place segments on baking sheet lined with wax paper and store, covered, in the refrigerator to harden.

Just before serving, place frozen grapes in the middle of a platter. Surround with chocolate-dipped orange segments. *Serves 6.*

TIP: You can microwave chocolate (in a glass bowl or measure) on HIGH for 30 seconds, stir, then continue at 30 second intervals until melted.

DESSERTS

Poached Pears

Serve with Ginger Cookies and a dessert cheese.

> INGREDIENTS:
> 4 firm ripe pears, peeled, cored (from the bottom), stems intact
> 3 tablespoons fresh lemon juice
> 1 small strip lemon rind
> ½ teaspoon ground cloves
> ½ cup sugar
> ½ cup red wine or cranberry juice
>
> EQUIPMENT:
> 2-quart covered saucepan

Brush pears with lemon juice and set aside. In saucepan, place remaining juice and all other ingredients. Cook over high heat 1 minute, then stir and cook an additional minute or until sugar is dissolved. Stand pears in the mixture and baste them with the sauce. A bulb baster does this job well. Cover and simmer 12 minutes, basting every 3 minutes. Test for doneness, pears should be tender enough to be easily pierced with a fork. Let pears cool in their liquid, basting occasionally. Serve chilled or at room temperature. Nutmeg-laced whipped cream or plain yogurt can be served on the side. *Serves 4.*

Ginger Cookies

INGREDIENTS:
¼ cup butter or margarine
½ cup firmly packed light or dark brown sugar
½ cup dark molasses
3 ½ cups all-purpose flour
1 teaspoon baking soda
1 teaspoon ground cinnamon
2 teaspoons ground ginger
¼ teaspoon nutmeg
Pinch of salt
⅓ cup water

EQUIPMENT:
2 medium (2 ½-quart) mixing bowls
Rolling pin
Cookie sheet

In bowl, cream together butter and brown sugar; beat in molasses. Combine flour, baking soda, spices and salt in other bowl. Add to sugar mixture one-third at a time, alternating with water Stir until blended. Form dough into ball; cover with plastic wrap and refrigerate 3 hours.

Preheat oven to 350°. Roll out dough to ¼ inch thickness on lightly floured surface. Cut out cookies in desired shapes. Bake for 12 to 15 minutes on greased or nonstick cookie sheet. Cool on rack. *Yield: about 2 dozen cookies.*

Royal Meringue with Berries

This is a most unusual meringue. It has a custard like consistency and is baked in a bain marie or water bath.

INGREDIENTS:
- 10 egg whites
- ¾ teaspoon cream of tartar
- 1¼ cups sugar
- Dash almond extract
- 2 pints fresh strawberries, raspberries, or the equivalent amount of chopped fresh peaches (you may substitute frozen fruit, well drained.
- ¼ teaspoon almond extract, or dark rum if using peaches
- Sugar to taste

EQUIPMENT:
- Large (4 quart) mixing bowl
- Electric mixer
- 8-inch square baking pan
- Deep roasting pan
- Food processor or blender

Preheat oven to 300°. In bowl, beat egg white with cream of tartar until foamy. Slowly add sugar and beat until very thick. Fold in almond extract and spoon into baking pan. Bake in a bain marie: Set in a larger pan and add hot water to come halfway up the sides of the inner pan.

Bake 1 hour. Remove pan from water bath and set on a rack to cool. Meringue will fall slightly as it cools.

Place berries in food processor or blender. Add a little sugar (or not, according to taste) plus almond extract or rum. Pulse into a coarse puree. Spool meringue onto individual serving plates and top with berry mixture. *Serves 6.*

VARIATION: If you don't mind the calories or fat, fold 1 cup of lightly whipped cream into the berry mixture.

DESSERTS

Rhubarb Crisp

INGREDIENTS:
3 cups diced rhubarb
¾ cup sugar
¼ cup water
½ cup (1 stick) butter or margarine
1 cup firmly packed brown sugar
1¼ cups all-purpose flour

EQUIPMENT:
2 medium (2 ½-quart) mixing bowls
8-inch square baking dish
Pastry blender

Preheat oven to 350°. Mix rhubarb, sugar, and water in a bowl and place in greased baking dish. In second bowl, cut butter into brown sugar and flour, using pastry blender, until mixture is crumbly, Spread crumbs over rhubarb and bake 40 minutes, or until crumb topping is lightly browned and rhubarb is tender. Serve warm or cold, plain, or with cream or ice cream. *Serves 4 to 6.*